Living with Bipolar Disorder:
My Story about Rising to the Top of My Game and Hitting the Bottom of Despair

by
E. Fiske-Jorgensen

"Before you start to judge me, step into my shoes and walk the life I'm living, and if you get as far as I am, just maybe you will see how strong I am." ~ unknown

Table of Contents

Introduction

This book is about my own personal triumphs and struggles with Bipolar Disorder, coupled with ADHD. I have found some good books and articles about the disorder; but unfortunately, there is still a great deal left unknown about it, even among the most educated in the field. So it is quite an undertaking to find anything to help further your understanding of it or how to cope with it. Along those same lines, very few people are willing to tell their story, mainly because of the stigmas attached to it.

The primary reason I wrote this book is to help others struggling with Bipolar Disorder. Perhaps, if you have been diagnosed with it, you can find a gold nugget along the way that is helpful, or perhaps you can relate to my entire story. The other reason for writing my story is to help me find some clarity and a better comprehension of what I now have to manage for the rest of my life.

If you are reading this to help someone you love with Bipolar Disorder, I hope that this book will help you to grasp it a little better, but be cautious in knowing that each person has his or her own struggles and stories to tell. This book is just *my story*.

I purposefully omitted all names from the book for confidentiality purposes and to respect others' privacy. Nothing detracts from the stories, but once you read them, you will understand my reasons for this decision.

Throughout the book, I also share some valuable resources that I have found along the way that have helped me better understand and cope with the disorder. I hope they help you too.

Chapter 1:
Childhood

I was not diagnosed with Bipolar II until the age of 42, which is quite a late diagnosis. But as I think back through my childhood and early adult experiences, I can clearly pinpoint episodes and behavioral examples that highlight the disorder. So, I wanted to start this chapter with a few of the earliest memories I have of my childhood to illustrate symptoms of the disorder and progress to the end of high school.

My Early School Years

The first day of kindergarten is supposed to be one of most exciting things to happen by the time you reach age five or six. But for me, it was horrifying! As a little girl, I would hide behind one of parent's legs when someone approached to say hello, and I did not respond to them when they paid any attention to me.

There were a few kids in my neighborhood I played with before going off to kindergarten, but most of the time I preferred playing alone. What I had going on in my own head always seemed far more fascinating, and excluding the outside world also provided a sense of comfort to me.

I remember when my mom walked me to the classroom on that first day of kindergarten. All I wanted to do was run back to the car and go home. There was this new place, full of new kids and a teacher I had never met. Most of the kids were very joyful and playing with each other. That is when I first truly realized that I was different from others. Why were they so excited, and why was I so terrified?

My parents always thought of me as their introverted child. But, it is more complicated than that, as featured writer by *New York Times, Time, and Psychology Today*, Susan Cain discusses in her recent book, *Quiet: the Power of Introverts in a World that Can't Stop Talking*. She contends that introversion is a preference for environments and events that are not over-stimulating, while shyness is the fear of social disapproval or humiliation. I was and am *both* shy and introverted.

Shyness is basically social anxiety, whereas introversion is not. One reason the two concepts get confused is because sometimes they overlap. Social anxiety, or shyness, is only about people, while introversion is about new places or events. Unfortunately, I am quite introverted with a fairly high-level of social anxiety or shyness. This means that new people, new places, and new events *all* create a sense of angst and discomfort for me.

One way to put it is that I prefer to "live in my own head". Any attention I was given as a child, I considered bad attention. I did nothing to get in trouble, nor did I try to excel. But, I could analyze and solve problems faster than other kids; they just did not know it, nor did my teachers or parents.

I would work my way through each grade around the middle of the pack, always known as the shy kid, but never showing anyone what I could really do and what I really knew. In our 3rd grade school play, I even had to play the part of Flower in Bambi, the timid skunk character. My brothers loved the fact I had to play the role of a skunk. I was just glad I only had one speaking part in the whole play.

As I mentioned, I was very shy along with being an introvert. I felt awkward and apprehensive when others approached me, and I had no coping mechanisms to deal with it, especially as a kid. I always felt very uncomfortable in different places or at new events.

What I truly loved was being at home and alone, because I always felt more energized and happy with whatever I was doing by myself, and I never had to worry about everything and everyone else around me.

Right before I was born, my parents designed and built a five-level, 16 room house, where from the front entrance, you could get to any room in the home without going through another room. It was truly a unique design, and I used it to my advantage to avoid people and situations.

The front entrance was actually the third-level of the house. When someone I did not want to interact with came to the front door, I would scramble up the stairs to the fourth floor, down the hallway, and crawl into the laundry chute, where I would shimmy down to the second floor to the top of the dryer. From there, I would sneak out of the laundry room, into the game room, and then head out the back door. It was also not uncommon for me to hide-out in cabinets or closets.

One early childhood story that illustrates my social anxiety and introversion occurred when I was somewhere between ages five and seven. I went with my dad to a new home site. He was a professor, but he designed and built houses in the summer for extra money. I had to go with him to a home site one day, because my mom had other plans. My dad thought I would like the new park right across the street where other kids were usually playing.

We arrived at the job site, and I found a place on the curb to sit. I saw the park and other kids playing, but I did not give much thought to joining in their games. As my dad and his work crew started their job, I began to watch what they were doing and how they were doing it. At the same time, I was entertaining myself with my own thoughts. Occasionally, my dad would wave at me or do something funny to make me laugh.

Pretty soon a girl about my age came up and asked me to come over to the park to play. I told her "No, I have to stay with my dad." Then, I turned back around and went back to watching and thinking.

I did not have to stay with my dad. I just did not want to go play with her or play with the other kids. It was not only the kids, but it was a new park I had never been to before, and I was uncomfortable leaving my place on the curb. I was watching and learning how to build a house, and my mind was in another world that was far more entertaining than the park games across the street.

While most kids would be bored and jump at the chance to go to the park and interact with other children, I chose to sit quietly by myself. Once the morning was over, my dad took me back home. He asked why I did not go play at the park. I said, "Just didn't want to." That was all he asked and the end of that discussion.

When I was a young teenager, my mom and I were in the middle of a discussion about my childhood. During that conversation, I remember her telling me that I did not like to be touched or held as a baby or toddler, especially by unfamiliar people. So apparently, human interaction was discomforting to me even then.

I had two older brothers, both fairly outgoing, and I was aware that I was different from them. As a very young child, I thought it was a gender issue. Boys were sociable and liked to interact with the world, and girls were shy and liked to be left alone. As I grew a little older, I realized this was not the case. I was just very different from most other kids.

Overall, my childhood was pretty good, but it was unique. I was a "tomboy" and liked to play football and rough-house with the younger of my two brothers, who was less than two years older than me. He passed away at the young age of 35 from cancer, and I miss him dearly. I always felt like he was the only person in my life who was always in my corner no matter the circumstance. But, now I feel that he is watching over me, and I find comfort in that through the rough times.

Junior High & High School

Junior high was when I began to find trouble. School was just too boring, and the teen years were knocking. I would find other things to do in and outside of the classroom to entertain my brain, of which most teachers did not find amusing.

Underneath all the quietness was a keen sense of humor, which I used to make friends. I inherited that from my dad, who was often compared to Steve Martin when I was growing up. My dad is very outgoing, and his sense of humor shines all of the time. He can make anyone laugh!

My sense of humor surfaces in far more reserved ways, through pranks or quiet smart remarks. But, we both tend to find the same things funny, and our connection is through our sense of humor and also our intellect.

Junior high is also when I began to realize there are loopholes in just about everything, much like the laundry chute I used as a child. I began to master the art of finding those loopholes. Sometimes, it did not always work out, so I would get into some sort of trouble. This is where my parents shifted their thoughts from me, not only being their "shy kid", but also their "troublemaker".

While I never intended to cause any harm, I needed to find ways to keep my brain occupied. School was not able to do that, as I found most things easy to learn the first time around. I rarely read my textbooks, and if I did, it was once-through and fairly quickly.

I made it through high school without getting into too much trouble. I only had one in-school suspension, which meant nothing to me. They thought isolation was punishment. To me, it was a gift.

Chapter 2:
College Life

This chapter focuses on how I got through college, all the way from my freshman year through my Ph.D. program. Sometimes I still wonder how I managed it all, because it was all done in such a strange and unique manner. But, somehow I reached every stepping stone along the way, which ultimately led to my career.

Being an Undergraduate

I started college at a larger public university a few hundred miles from where I grew up. One reason I chose that school was because all my friends were going to other universities, and I wanted to test myself out in an environment where I knew no one. I had a sense, at a very deep level, that I needed to do this but I was not sure why. The university I chose seemed to fit the profile.

My parents dropped me off, helped me unpack my things, and left for their new home about 400 miles away in a new city and state. There I was, all alone in a much larger city than where I graduated high school, and at university of which I had very little knowledge.

I found out very quickly just how unskilled and uncomfortable I was with new places and new people. I had no friends the first semester, and I do mean none! I had a roommate, but she was "weird". I did not talk to anyone in my classes. I did not join any clubs. I did not know how or even want to be a part of any group. Classes were not challenging like I was told they would be, so I took my textbooks back to the book store and returned them for beer money.

While I had not made any friends, I did not find myself to be too lonely. I liked being alone, and I had so much going on inside my head that it continually kept me occupied and entertained. My roommate was gone every weekend, so it was perfect for drinking beer and being alone with my thoughts.

During the second semester of my freshman year, a girl down the hall befriended me. I liked her immediately, because she had scotch and cigarettes in her top desk drawer. She also had a way of bringing out my sense of humor, which was the one thing I was missing. We taught each other our favorite pranks, and we certainly had more than our fair share of fun together.

The rest of our gang was pretty small, which I liked. The five of us spent our time drinking, smoking, and playing pranks on everyone else in the dorm. So, I did find enjoyment through them during those times.

That first college friend and I still keep in touch, and we often reminisce about our college days. Unfortunately, I only had two semesters with her and our posse, the spring of my freshman year and the fall of my sophomore year.

That fall semester I got a DWI, and my father gave me an ultimatum. I either had to finish my studies where he was teaching, at a small Midwestern university; or I could stay in the Southwest where I was, but he would cut me off. I was a smart enough girl to know I needed to finish my education, so I chose to go the Midwest the spring of my sophomore year.

Once again, I was headed off to a place where I knew no one (it was not where I grew up) and did not really care to make friends, as I was very bitter about the move. I quickly realized that I did not care too much for the Midwest, as it was pretty boring and far too cold.

The next fall semester, I started dating a guy I met at a keg party. His friends just naturally became my friends. I also took a job at local department store, one of the few places to get a job in such a small town. I made friends with a couple of the girls who worked there, but nothing very substantial.

I finished my undergraduate degree as soon as I could, which was in three years (1½ already finished at the first university), then I went straight into a master's degree program. That took one year, and during that year, I decided to get my Ph.D.

Beginning the Ph.D. Program

I transferred from one of the small university system campuses to the much larger flagship campus, where the number of students enrolled was greater than the population of the town where I was residing. I was now 23 years old and starting my Ph.D., where I commuted back and forth each week, two hours each way.

I was still dating the same guy, which is one reason I chose to stay in the Midwest a few more years and deal with the commute. I think he liked how busy I was, because it meant he had more time to hunt and fish. But, we did have good relationship, and he was a great guy. However, that relationship did not last, nor was it meant to be, but I will talk more about that later.

As I mentioned earlier, I learned at a young age that there are loopholes in just about everything. The Ph.D. program was no exception. I used my dad's knowledge as a professor and my own "know-how" to find those loopholes. I heard from most of my professors and peers that it took five to six years to complete the Ph.D. program. That seemed way too long, so I figured out a way to finish in just three years.

Just shy of my 26th birthday, I walked the stage at graduation and was hooded a doctorate. But before getting to that, I need to spend some time on how I managed to get through the Ph.D. program.

Managing the Ph.D. Program

Getting a Ph.D. meant teaching classes, taking classes with others in my cohort, conducting research, and getting to know all my professors on several levels, along with a few other ins-and-outs. It was no easy task, and it all took a major toll on me, mentally and emotionally. In fact, I had my first panic attack during my Ph.D. program, but I had no idea what had happened to me until much later when I learned what they are and their symptoms.

While I am an introvert, I appear to be an extrovert in the classroom. There is something about standing up in front of a group of people, who I may or may not know, that tends to alter that trait in me. I am not sure how this happens when I find it so hard to establish one-on-one relationships or fit well into small groups.

While I still do not fully grasp it today, there is some sort of "disconnect" for me. The atmosphere is structured and familiar, and relationships are not personal because of the classroom setting and nature of the roles. That disconnect allows me to excel at teaching and receive very good evaluations from the students.

While I have become better over the past several years with personal student relationships, I still prefer larger than smaller classes, because there is less intimacy and need for one-on-one interaction. I do not form close bonds with my students. That type of disconnect, created by the nature of our roles, is essential for my success.

In my Ph.D. Program, the average class size in the courses we took ranged from 9-12 students. They were conducted seminar-style, where everyone sat around the table and discussed the material for the day, including the professor. While I participated, this was not up my alley at all. By the time the class ended, I needed my alone time.

Most of the cohort would go out to lunch together or go for happy hour if the class was later in the day, but I would pass almost every time. I know they sensed something was different about me, and they began to treat me like an outcast during the middle of my first semester. That was a scenario I created myself, and I was okay with this; however, I was concerned it would interfere with my success in the program, but ultimately it did not.

My advisor even had at talk with me one day about not bonding with the cohort and going home every weekend. He tried to convince me to change my behaviors, but that was not in my plan to get out as quickly as possible. I continued to get by with my established behaviors, because I had a good relationship with him, even though he was considered to be *very* tough. His ratings on research papers were among only three categories, "total crap", "crap", or "not crap".

I had to learn that "not crap" meant that it was a really good paper. I am a very high-achiever and do not consider feedback less than superb to be anything of value. So, I had to ingrain into my mind that "not crap" meant that I had done a great job.

I only received one paper with "total crap" written on it. That was very devastating moment and quite a learning experience. There was literally more red ink on that paper than the words I had typed out in black.

I found a connection with an Eastern European guy who no one else in the cohort liked. He was extremely abrasive towards people, but he was a genius, especially when it came to statistics. To me, he was by far the most interesting person in the cohort.

We would eat lunch together about twice a week, which consisted of three or four beers, a few cigarettes, along with some food at a local brewpub that we really could not afford at the time. We would talk about research at great lengths and at levels we never reached in the classroom. I think we both realized we were the most intelligent ones in our cohort, which further strengthened our bond. I learned many things about statistics from him that we never discussed in our classes.

At night, we would frequent a local jazz bar, where we drank gin, smoked cigarettes, and made fun of Midwestern people trying to dance to jazz music. During these outings our conversations were more personal than professional, but never at a level where it felt uncomfortable for either one of us.

The Ph.D. cohort thought there was more to our relationship than there was, but we really did not care. He was happily engaged; and at the time, I was happy with my relationship two hours down the road. After a stellar night of gin and cigarette consumption, we could still pass exams and complete projects at levels that exceeded our peers' output.

I lived in an efficiency apartment, which was perfect for my personality traits and work demands. I did not want a roommate or to live on campus. I would spend all my time reading textbooks, along with stacks and stacks of research papers. Most of it was assigned, but some was extra material I picked up myself. I knew with my nightlife activities, I had to figure out a better way to get through the material faster and with a higher comprehension rate. I relied back on a one-hour class I taught during my master's program on speed reading.

I eventually taught myself to read 1,000 words per minute, with about an 85% comprehension rate. I slowed that down a tad to achieve a 95+% comprehension rate, so I could master the knowledge of each and every article and book I read. Unfortunately, this practice led to a very serious problem for me at one point called Spondylitis, which is basically inflammation in the vertebrae joints.

I woke up one morning after a long night of reading, and I literally could not move my neck. The inflammation had caused bulging discs and pinched nerves. I was in so much pain that it was unbearable to even sit upright.

I found out, after a visit to the doctor, that I had caused this myself by reading for several hours at a time with my head locked in a lowered position. After working to decrease the inflammation, the nerves and discs began to feel much better. But, I had to learn to take breaks about every thirty-minutes of reading and to keep my spine aligned while working on the computer.

Taking breaks is still something I have to be cognizant of today, because I can read and write for hours at a time without thinking about it. But, I do know that I never want to feel that kind of pain again, so it has become a routine. However, during hypomanic episodes, I have to *force* myself to do it or at least stretch out.

The Deep Rooting of Depression

Depression was something that began taking on deep roots during the first year of the program. I did not recognize it as depression then, but that is what I was experiencing. I honestly thought I had some sort of physical problem like Mono or something. I would find myself very fatigued, not wanting to go to class, and almost sick at the thought of interacting with people, especially in those seminar classes.

One day, I found the very bottom floor of the library, where very few dared to go. It was down three or four flights of stairs, where they housed older versions of psychology and sociology journals. On most days I was the only one down there. If anyone else was ever there, it was a rare sighting.

This was my haven to get away from it all, and I mean everything. It was so quiet and eerily vacant, but it was a place for no human interaction, and the environment became more and more comforting each time I went down there.

Usually, I would study my school material, but at other times I found myself digging through some of the psychology journals trying to find out what was wrong with me. I never found anything that fit what I was experiencing, so I would just use that library space to sleep, read, and try to gather some energy to get through the day.

On my two-hour drives back and forth on weekends, I was always immersed in deep thought about why I was so different from my peers, and I would also make a plan for how to get through the weekend by splitting ample time between my boyfriend and my workload.

I don't think my family ever picked up on my depression. For one thing, emotions were not something easily shared. In fact, it was somewhat "taboo" in my family. They just thought I had a ton of work to do and never bothered me.

The drive back to school on Monday mornings was dreadful, as I would awaken at 4am to make it to my 8am class to teach. Some days I just wanted to pull over and sleep, but that was not an option. Mondays were the most grueling days during the program, but somehow I managed them.

Finding the Loopholes & Finishing Early

During the end of my second year, I knew I needed to get out of that place. I hated the Midwest, felt unhappy most of the time, and never meshed with my Ph.D. cohort. I began to strategize a plan to get out early by finding a loophole in the system.

My advisor had done a research study that resulted in a book publication he was very proud to display and discuss. So, my idea was to approach him about doing my dissertation by utilizing the same methodological approach he used in his book, except on a different population of people; and best of all, we could use the results for a comparative study.

He thought it was a great idea and bought into it very quickly. His "buy-in" allowed me to begin my dissertation work before the standard time when this was allowed, according to the rules of the program. But with his approval, that became my primary focus, as I was handling the class work just fine.

I had the study designed and ready to go in a short period of time. My advisor had seniority over all the other professors, so he allowed me to begin gathering the data during my third year, which "technically" I was not supposed to do. This did *not* make my peers and some of the other professors very happy. But, at that point I really did not care.

The project progressed quickly and I had all my data gathered as soon as I could manage. Then, it was time for statistical analysis. My Eastern European friend helped tremendously during this phase of the study, and by the end of the third year, I had my dissertation complete. Finishing up my last semester of classes, I was riding high on my laurels and knew I just had to stick it out until the end.

The oral comprehensive exam was at the end of the last semester of coursework. Some of the professors wanted me to fail, because of the way my dissertation was handled and I was only a third year student. During the exam, there was no question that stumped me, except for one random one. My advisor also picked up on the tension in the room, and thankfully, squashed it. So, oral comps were done and I passed with flying colors. Now it was time to defend my dissertation.

I had to defend in front on the same group of professors. Unfortunately, my weak spot was statistics. They hammered me on that. But, everything in my dissertation supported my findings. It was all there, I just felt that I had not explained it to their satisfaction. Where was my Eastern European friend when I needed him? I thought they had found my Achilles' heel and I was doomed to fail.

After your defense, you are asked to wait out in the hallway while they discuss whether or not to pass or fail you. After a long wait, my advisor came out of the room, extended his hand, and said, "Congratulations, you passed." I was shocked and overjoyed!

As I walked back to my office another professor followed me. I opened my door to put my things away. He stuck his head in and said, "If it were up to me, you would fail. There is something off about this whole dissertation, and there is just something *off about you*." Wow! I was stunned and had nothing to say back to him. He then turned around and left.

After pondering his comments for a few moments, I reminded myself that I was done and that he no longer had any control over me or my work. I was out of there! In just a few weeks I would be granted a Ph.D.

Chapter 3:
My Career

This chapter focuses on getting back to Southwest to start my career and all the hoops I had to jump through to get my promotions. It also focuses on the downside to my strategies and manners of doing this. My never-ending drive, along with my lack of knowledge about my psychological disorders, led to my ever-growing feelings of depression, inferiority, and social anxiety. This ultimately led to a state of pure despair, all of which I discuss throughout this chapter.

Starting My Career

With a Ph.D. in hand, my goal was to get the hell out of the Midwest and back to my old stomping grounds. Unfortunately, when I graduated there was only one job in the nation for every five people looking in my area of specialization. This did not bode well, and I thought that through my dad's connections, I might be stuck teaching at his university for awhile.

But one day the phone rang, and it was a university located in the Southwest calling me because they found my profile in a database of recent graduates looking for jobs. Fortunately, I had something they needed, which was a unique combination of the ability to teach in two somewhat unrelated areas. One area was my degree specialization and the other was the topic of my dissertation. I quickly agreed to an interview. Luckily, I got the job!

Very much to my relief, I would be heading back down South. This move put my relationship in question. While he had always supported by education and career, he had no desire to move away from the Midwest.

Our relationship lasted less than one year after my move and new career began. He promised to look for jobs where I was working but never did. Instead, he bought an engagement ring with the hopes that I would find a job back in the Midwest and marry him. This led to our break up, because I was not about to do something so drastic that we had not even discussed, and I was not moving back to the Midwest! I also felt that he had not lived up to his promises.

That ended a six-year relationship. It was a hard thing for everyone, as he had become so much a part of my family, and he and my brother had become and remained best friends. But, I knew it was the right thing for me. I also started questioning my sexuality. That is not a topic I will delve into in this book, but while I do like men, I prefer women. A few years later, I met my life partner, and we have been together now for over 11 years. I will introduce her later on in this chapter.

Climbing the Career Ladder

I started my career at a small, private, and fairly prominent school. Naturally, my thoughts were on getting tenure. I was told that, while you could technically go up for tenure in four years, it was not advisable until your sixth year. Of course, I went up in four years and got it (love those loopholes), along with being promoted to associate professor.

The one rule where I could not find a loophole was in being granted full-professor. You had to have 12 full years of experience under your belt, and there was no way around that. Unfortunately, I never learned how to make make time disappear.

Twelve years seemed like forever, which was really only eight at that point, since I was promoted to associate professor after my fourth year. But, I worked to exceed all expectations in teaching, research and service. So, when it was my time, I was unanimously voted in as full-professor.

I had spent the past 15 years jumping through hoops to get the Ph.D., a job, tenure, and my promotions; and now there was nowhere else to go, unless I chose the administrative route. As an administrator, you can work your way up from department chair, to dean, to vice president, and eventually president of a university. But, that is not me. Nothing about that route is appealing.

It would mean, no more teaching, much less to do with research and writing, and much more to do with people problems and networking, all of which would lead to my ever-increasing social anxiety and take away from my much-needed alone time.

Despair Despite the Achievements

The summer after being promoted to full-professor was filled with doubt, depression, and confusion. I had no goals ahead of me, no more hoops to jump through, and no more loopholes to find. I was only 38 years old, with about thirty more years to go in this profession.

I began to question what I had done to myself and why I was so hell-bent on getting through everything so quickly. I had time to look at myself in a more profound way than I had ever done so in the past, but ultimately it led back to the age-old question of, "Why was I so different from everyone else?" just as I had pondered that first day of kindergarten.

I began to feel inferior in so many ways, despite my achievements. I constantly wondered what was wrong with me. I was thinking about the chaotic nature in which my life operated compared to others. I could get so much done, and accomplished so well, but always in such a state of complete disarray.

I continued to wonder why I needed so much time alone, and why I could not connect with people like others were able to do. I also noticed my social anxiety was increasing even more. I began avoiding social gatherings and networking functions all together, unless alcohol was heavily involved. It was a long and difficult summer with no answers to any of these questions.

Three years after being granted full-professor, I was given one more promotion to an endowed chair position. While that carries a more significant status, nothing really changed regarding the job role itself, with the exception of serving as a mentor to junior faculty members. So, at age 41, I was truly at the top of my career game, yet still one of the youngest ones teaching at the university.

However, all of the same questions were still abound. What am I going to do for the next 30 years to excel and remain interested and happy in a productive manner? I began to drink even more to squash out those thoughts and quiet my worries. It also helped decrease my social anxiety and self-doubt. At this point I could hardly stand to be at any gathering with more than about six to eight people without the help of alcohol.

I started to convince myself that it was some sort of physical problem. But, I knew deep down there was much more to it. I knew had a serious psychological problem for years that I had never dealt with. But yet, I decided to lean on my title and the accomplishments I had on paper to convince myself that I was fine.

Alcohol

Since alcohol has come up a few times thus far, I will begin to address it here. It was huge part of my life. As a kid, we had beer at almost every high school party. That was just the norm. It was easy to come by in college, and I always had it on-hand as an adult. I never saw a problem with drinking. It was just a part of me and the only thing that slowed my ever-churning thoughts.

As I mentioned before, I had to move to the Midwest because of a DWI. Interestingly, I got another DWI my first semester at that little Midwestern school. So, my dad knew then that he had not solved that problem. There is actually a lot of drinking there, because it is cold and not much else to do. I remember, on more than one occasion, getting absolutely hammered the night before an exam and then acing it the next morning, all the while trying not to vomit on the floor.

When I started my job as a professor, I would buy cases of beer at the liquor store. I had my beer each and every night, and not just a few. While I never taught class drunk, I was hungover more times than not.

I was also at a university that liberally supported alcohol consumption at almost all events. So, I was surrounded and supported by my heavy-drinking colleagues. Once again, I saw nothing wrong with it. It was just a part of my day, like brushing my teeth or combing my hair. What I did not realize, at the time, was that I was using alcohol on a daily-basis to self-medicate my mounting psychological problems.

Love is in the Air

I met my life partner four years after I started my career. She was it! She had everything I was looking for, and we even met on the Internet, when meeting like that was considered strange and dangerous. She was the head basketball coach at another local university.

Aside from our careers, we had many things in common. We both liked sports, beer, traveling, movies, had the same sense of humor, and we both have very eclectic tastes in music. She had a unique look, was extremely fit, and has beautiful blue eyes that light up when she smiles. I also liked that she is fairly quiet. Most women like to talk more than I ever care to entertain. What I did not know at the time was that she had a serious problem with alcohol. And I say that without an ounce of criticism, because I too can be considered an alcoholic.

We drank together every day. In fact, it was a big part of our connection. We even planned road trips around brewpubs and breweries, and we joined every drinking club in town. This went on for three years until she lost her job. Then, I saw what hitting rock bottom really looks like. She sat on the couch for six months and drank. She was not drinking beer though; instead, she was drinking vodka along with other hard liquor.

After six months of that I told her to get off the couch and get a job. She resented me for making her do it. But, I could not stand it any longer. Disappointingly, she did not go back to a university position. She ended up in retail. For some reason, I looked down on that. She was my other half, a reflection of me. I felt that retail was beneath her education-level and capabilities. But, it beat drinking vodka on the couch all day, so I let it go.

The drinking went back to "normal", meaning we went back to drinking a case beer every night, and left the vodka for a happy hour every once in awhile.

Chapter 4:
My Unraveling Health Problems

This chapter discusses how my health problems began to unravel on me, and rather quickly. I was not feeling well most of the time. I attributed much of it to my weight gain, but I also knew there was more to it than just that. As I began to explore this with a basic annual physical (which I had skipped a few years), other things began to unfold in the psychological realm, leading to my diagnoses of Bipolar II and ADHD.

As I described in the last chapter, my use of alcohol to dissolve the despair in my life was becoming more of a problem. I used alcohol to escape my ever-churning thoughts, as I had no other way to control them along with numbing my feelings of pure anguish.

One thing I was not feeling positive about either was my physical appearance. Being in a relationship where both of us drank, the weight packed on little by little each year. In time, we each found ourselves to be overweight by at least 20 pounds or more and decided to try to get back in shape.

Getting into Physical Shape

Most people have at least heard of CrossFit by now, but if you have not, I will explain it to you in a nutshell. By definition, it is an exercise program based on functional (running, jumping, pulling, throwing), high-intensity movements. There are also weights involved, some basic gymnastics, and cardiovascular movements like running and rowing.

We chose the CrossFit method for getting back into physical shape, as opposed to doing it on our own at your standard gym. It is a very different type of workout routine and also a unique atmosphere, to say the least. We felt at the time that it would provide the right foundation and support for meeting our fitness goals.

As we soon discovered, The CrossFit community is one of *extremists*! They take their workouts (called wods) very seriously. In fact, most will say it is not an exercise program, but a lifestyle. That is true of their eating habits as well, as most adhere to the Paleo Diet, which consists of lean meats, green veggies, fruit, nuts, and seeds. There are no starchy vegetables like rice or white potatoes, no sugar, and no bread. While there is a significant amount of science behind the Paleo diet, there is no need to go into it.

CrossFitters can even be somewhat arrogant to those who do not follow their exercise and diet programs, and they often monitor each other for faults. Some people call it a cult, and while I will not go that far, it might not be too far off in some circles.

During the week, Monday morning until Saturday night, CrossFitters obey the lifestyle. They are working very hard in the gym four to six days each week and eating Paleo meals 80+% of the time. It is pretty hardcore! The workouts are grueling, and if you are not a competitive person or a high-achiever, CrossFit is not for you. The results are pretty amazing though. A true CrossFitter's body beats any fitness magazine's cover body. They even have the International CrossFit Games, which airs on ESPN, and the live event sells out every year.

But there is another extreme to CrossFit, as we knew it, and that was the Saturday night partying. A CrossFit party puts any frat party to shame. We would either have a party at someone's house or go out, and I'll describe each of those scenarios.

The owners of the gym would host most of the parties. If a keg of beer was not ordered, then everyone would just bring a case or two of beer. Those people who did not bring beer, brought bottles of tequila, vodka, or other hard liquor. Parties would start around 9pm and end around sunrise. Every last drop of alcohol in the house was consumed, along with all the food in sight. Group sizes would range from 15 to sometimes 40 people. Most would go home at some point during the night, but about six to eight would usually stay through the night.

As the drinking began and everyone loosened up, a lot of improper sexual activity occurred. No one even questioned it. But, when you have a house full of drunken people with fabulous bodies, something is bound to go down.

Most things that occurred were considered harmless. But, nonetheless, kissing, touching, and groping between people who were not in a relationship or in a relationship with someone else (even married) occurred at most occasions. While most things happened in a fairly harmless manner right in the middle of the party, there were nights when all the bedrooms were occupied, but not for sleeping. Waking up with someone you did not arrive at the party with was not uncommon for some people.

Going out was another story. Normally, we would start off at a restaurant where we would eat copious amounts of food, generally in parties of 12-20 people. The drinking would start before the appetizers, of course. By the end of the meal, it was not uncommon for the manager to tell us to quiet down. We even got kicked out of one restaurant.

Much to my embarrassment, we were not high school or college kids, but adults in our late-20s to early 40s. I usually felt bad for families that sat near us, and I was always concerned about running into a student or colleague, which did happen on a couple of somewhat sticky occasions.

From the restaurant, the party generally moved to a club, where we would take over the dance floor and the drinking would continue until one of the guys got into a fight or we were just ready to leave. But, no one ever wanted to go home. So, where do you go at 2am? A strip club, of course.

There were a couple of strip clubs we frequented and normally stayed until close. Lewd behavior among the entire group was the norm. Our girls looked so much better than any of the girls on stage, so they would perform some interesting acts for both our guys and girls, as bisexual curiosity was not uncommon or even questioned.

The interesting thing about this group was that you would never expect this kind of behavior to occur from any of us outside of those Saturday nights. The group mainly consisted of career-oriented professionals, who were accountants, business owners, teachers, doctors, military personnel, managers, nurses, and the like. But, everyone acted as if we somehow deserved to indulge in such rogue behavior after a long work week and the rigid CrossFit regime.

Some of the behaviors I engaged in could have easily led to job loss for me, especially during the public strip club outings. But, I was at almost every party on those Saturday nights. It was such a huge distraction from my moments of despair, and I would get so completely annihilated on alcohol that it usually took the entire day after to recover. That left very little energy in my head for thinking.

Monday morning, everything went back to normal at the gym, with members committed to their exercise and diet programs. Not much was discussed about the party other than how much fun we had and couldn't wait until the next Saturday night.

I do want to clarify that I am _not_ speaking for all CrossFit gyms across the globe. But, I am purporting that the same philosophy and those behaviors held true at three different gyms, of which we were either members or somehow associated.

A few years into this CrossFit lifestyle and partying with the different gyms, my partner said "No more!" She just could not do it anymore. Life was about to change.

Life Takes a 180 Degree Turn

One Monday my partner walked out of the bedroom and said, "I'm done!" I asked, "Done with what?" She responded with, "Drinking! I can't do it anymore. I feel like my body is shutting down." I responded with an "ok" thinking that it would last two or three days. But, she was dead serious.

By not drinking, she began to experience very high levels of anxiety and physical illness. She soon became a person I did not even recognize. I kept trying to convince her to get some help. I knew of a therapist who dealt with alcoholism, and I tried to connect them on more than one occasion. But, she was not ready for help. This was all taking hold just as a new school year was beginning for me.

The next blow came when she said she had to step away from CrossFit. She just could not be around that whole "scene" under her condition and in her efforts to stop drinking. She was feeling sick most of the time, which does not make anyone want to be around people who are exercising or drinking. She soon quit her part-time coaching job at one of the local gyms.

We "lost" many friends during this time period. I put the word lost in quotes, because we really did not lose them as friends. It was just an "out of sight, out of mind" mentality on their part. We are the ones who left the gym, and neither of us could expect them to come knocking on our door. We have reconnected and remain good friends with most of them. We just do not engage in the whole CrossFit scene anymore.

My partner was just not getting better, mentally or physically. She started to miss worked regularly, and I would literally drive home from school wondering if I would find her dead or alive. I was worried that the combination of her physical and mental condition was serious enough to take its ultimate toll on her, or that she just might take her own life. So, my stress-level was through the roof.

I was also in the middle of trying to heal from a pretty bad foot injury at that time and was fairly immobile except for going to and from work. So, I was gaining weight again, my social circle was gone, my partner was very sick and almost unrecognizable, things were not going too well at work, and I had a shattered joint capsule and broken toe in my foot. All of this, in combination, led to even more drinking to manage the stress and pain.

The Results of My Physical

I decided to get an annual physical the following spring, and it was not good news. My results implied that I was a walking time bomb for a stroke or heart attack. I was overweight, had high blood pressure, high cholesterol, and my CRP level was quite high.

CRP stands for C-reactive protein. Basically, it is a protein found in your blood that rises in response to inflammation in the body. So, if you burned your hand on the stove, your CRP level would rise. I had no injury like that, so it meant only one thing, inflammation inside the body; and most likely, that inflammation was in the arteries. In sum, the coronary-risk of the combination of my results was not good, especially with a history of stroke in my family.

My doctor practically put me on a heart patient's diet, with less than 20 grams of fat per day. I thought to myself at the time, "Well, at least there's no fat in alcohol!" Exercise was on the to-do list as well. I had to drop some weight and focus on my health. I felt terrible, physically and mentally.

In the meantime, my partner was finally getting some counseling. And as I suspected, she really liked the therapist. She is firm, but caring. She takes your problems seriously, but also has a sense of humor. I knew my partner would like her if she just gave it a chance. I had used this counselor before when my brother was dying of cancer, and even though we only had a few sessions, I did take note that one of her specialties was alcoholism.

As time went on, my medical doctor also wanted me to get a handle on stress. The weight was coming off, but there were so many other factors that had changed in our lives that stress was having a major negative impact on me. I made an appointment with the same therapist my partner was seeing for her alcoholism. That turned into much more than I bargained for, because it ultimately led to my diagnoses of Bipolar II and ADHD.

My Diagnoses of Bipolar II & ADHD

My original intent with the therapy sessions was to lower my stress levels in order to achieve better physical health. I do not trust others easily, but I did trust her, so I found it bearable to devote an hour of one-on-one discussion with her each week. And I always left feeling better just by getting things off my chest.

But, one therapy session led to another, and as more and more came out, she threw me a loop. She said that, through our discussions and my writings, she was picking up on some things that led her to believe I might be ADHD or Bipolar II.

Next, she asked if I was willing to see a psychiatrist for an official diagnosis. I was taken by surprise, but I was willing to go, because I wanted to know. I always suspected I was a little ADD, but Bipolar II? I really did not know what that was at the time.

During my first appointment with my psychiatrist, I filled out all the paperwork, which seemed to take forever. After she read through everything, she asked me some very pointed questions about how my thought processes worked, along with how I handled certain work situations, social situations, and home situations, and then analyzed my responses.

By the end of that session, she had diagnosed me with both disorders, Bipolar II and ADHD, and both at a fairly high level. I left with a wholehearted sense of shock. At age 42, how am I just now finding this out? What does it all mean? And most of all, what is next?

Chapter 5:
Treatment & Acceptance

This chapter focuses on coming to terms with my newly diagnosed and lifelong disorders along with their treatments. I talk about accepting yourself as well as the acceptance of others. As I quickly learned, there are no "loopholes" with these illnesses like I had grown accustomed to finding and mastering throughout my lifetime. A new and brutal reality was now taking over my life.

The Treatment Begins

I shared the news of my diagnoses with my therapist, who was not terribly surprised. But, now we had to make a plan for how to deal with it. I learned that how I was used to functioning needed to drastically change, because the medications that I had been prescribed would not allow me to continue to function as I had for the past 40+ years. They were literally going to change how my brain worked!

That news was quite unsettling. How was I going to learn new ways to function that were practically the opposite of what I was used to doing before the diagnoses? It all seemed so sudden at first, like they found a cancerous tumor that had to be immediately removed.

At first, I was in complete denial. I was not going to accept that so many things had to change. I knew that I operated far different than most people, but I did *not* think of it as a disorder. I was outdoing most of my colleagues in the classroom, in research; and the day-to-day things, like paying the bills, were getting done. But, then I had to stop and consider all the things I did not do for myself, like dishes, laundry, and going to the grocery store. My partner took care of all that. Even when I had to travel for work, she would pack for me.

Packing takes me three to four hours to finish just for a weekend trip, because I get distracted with other things and also find it hard to focus on important factors, like the fact that you need to take along a coat to a colder climate. So, she just packs for me, and I considered this okay and normal. In fact, I think this was learned behavior from my childhood, as my mother took care of everything of this nature for us.

The next thing that came to mind was work! How would I function now? Would my success level plummet? Would I be seen as one of those professors to rise to the top just to sit back and do nothing? How would I ever hold my attention on a research paper that took two to three months to trudge through as opposed to hammering it out in four to five days during hypomania?

In therapy, one of the first things I had to learn was how to use a calendar. I had never even owned one, nor a watch for that matter. I kept everything in my head and relied on hypomania to push me through deadlines, and normally ahead of schedule. That is the way I had always functioned.

My therapist also began explaining how to break down large projects into smaller ones by making lists. Lists? I don't make lists! This was unfamiliar territory for me, and I was somewhat dejected at the thought of even trying it. In fact, it felt beneath me.

At times, I also felt so demoralized by the things my therapist had to explain to me, that it seemed the topics we were discussing were probably not too far off from what the third-graders down the road were learning. And it was not that these subjects and ideas were completely foreign to me, but they were the very things I now had to learn *how to do*.

After one of those sessions, I realized that I had to be *willing* to learn and change, because I had already started taking the prescribed medications to control both my Bipolar Disorder and ADHD. This would *require* me to learn how to function in a different way, because these medications were literally going to *change how my brain worked*. While my eyes and ears were open, my heart soul remained closed.

Giving up the Alcohol

The medications did not allow for alcohol, but I thought I could figure a way around that. There had be a "loophole" somewhere, right? During two or three incidents after I took my medications, I drank a few glasses of alcohol. And on those occasions, I became completely unable to function.

While I do not recall most of it, from what my partner described, it was very scary and bizarre. In fact, on one occasion I almost fell through the living room window and sustained some pretty substantial knots and bruising. I spent the next two weeks hiding an arm bruise from my therapist, which ran from my elbow all the way down to my wrist.

At about the same time, my general practitioner asked me to stop drinking for awhile. We had gone down the road to change my diet, start exercising, and get some stress-counseling. So, his next step was to eliminate the alcohol. He challenged me to 60 days, which seemed ridiculous at the time. But, I accepted it and was just going to wait for day 61.

After four to six weeks without alcohol, I realized I had to eliminate it from my life. It was not going to work with my medications, nor would it enhance my relationship with my partner, who now had her sights set on being sober for an entire year.

So, when day 61 rolled around, I knew that alcohol could no longer be a part of my life. It even fell on Thanksgiving Day, which we normally celebrated with champagne after a drinking a host of beer. As of today, I have been without alcohol for almost nine months but have not been without my temptations.

About thirty days into my sobriety, I was heading off for a weekend work-related retreat, where I knew the alcohol would be flowing, especially during the last night. In a couple's therapy session, I admitted that I was considering taking part in the drinking festivities. So, the rest of the session focused on me not being committed to the 60 days, and that if I did choose to drink, then my 60 days would have to start over. I was fairly angry after that session, because I was not the alcoholic. My partner was the alcoholic, so I thought at the time anyway.

My stubbornness is what kept me from drinking that weekend, because I simply wanted to prove my partner and my therapist to be wrong. Just because I was "considering" it did not mean I had already made up my mind to "do it", of which they were convinced I had. Most of the time my stubborn nature leads to no good, but in this instance, it served me well. I did not drink that weekend.

There have been a few other occasions in the last several months when I would have consumed alcohol if it were near me. Those times were in states of complete agitation or confusion over something I was trying to accomplish that was not going well. Fortunately, alcohol was nowhere nearby, so I have managed to stay sober. Of course, there is no alcohol in the house any longer. My wine rack for my wine club is gone. We even had to turn our cool sports bar into "just the game room".

I know that staying away from alcohol is the only way to go. But, I just hope I can continue down that path. My partner has been the biggest inspiration to me, as she has now been sober (with no relapses) for 15 months. Her internal strength provides the foundation for my will to stay sober. I also never want to let her down or cause her to relapse. That would be a worse-case scenario for the both of us.

One thing my therapist has talked to me about, on more than one occasion, is "quality of life". Basically, she just puts it out there like it really is. There is nothing I have to do or not do. I can choose to quit my therapy sessions or stop taking my medications. I can choose to drink or not to drink. All my decisions are mine alone to make, but I should always make them based on "quality of life".

Those discussions are another reason I have been able to stay away from the booze. I think back to our sessions and her words, and I know that my quality of my life on alcohol was nowhere near adequate or where it is today since eliminating it. I now understand that it was just my way of self-medicating before my unforeseen psychological diagnoses. And I also realize the negative impact it was having on me, both physically and mentally.

Who to Tell, Why, and How

Now you have a serious, lifelong medical condition. Part of acceptance is who to tell, understand why you are telling them, and to make a plan for how to tell them. We all know there are stigmas attached to Bipolar Disorder. It is not like telling someone you have an overactive thyroid.

When you tell someone you are Bipolar, you know the words that automatically come to mind – crazy, psycho, wacko, among others. And the media does not help by how they portray characters with mental disorders in movies or on TV shows. The fact is, Bipolar Disorder carries negative connotations with it, and there is no way around them.

First of all, you have to get over the self-stigma, the feeling that you are damaged, crazy, or somehow less than something you thought you were before the diagnosis. I am still struggling with this. I know it will take several therapy sessions to get me past the point where I think I can still be as productive and successful as I once was by utilizing newly learned behaviors. I am trying to get it all figured out and am making some progress. But, as of now, I still feel damaged and of less value than what I thought I was with hypomania.

I continue to remind myself that it is a *physiological* disorder and not something I created myself. That was one of the first things that I needed to learn. I had to read it several times, hear it from my psychiatrist, and hear it from my therapist, to get it drilled into my head that it is a genetic and physiological condition instead of something I created through my own decisions, thoughts, and behaviors.

I went through a period of self-blame, and I thought could overcome it. Those were two reasons I kept drinking, even on my medications. One reason was self-punishment, because I thought had caused these disorders. The second reason was simply to give less credence to the medications I was given to control my disorders.

Another thing everyone with Bipolar Disorder needs to realize is that not everyone has to know! You are same person the day before your diagnosis, as you are the day of your diagnosis, and every day after that. But, your behaviors *do* change as a result of the medications, and people who are frequently around you *will* notice these changes. This is especially true when your doctor is trying to find the right medications, as your behaviors and moods fluctuate. You have to be ready for the questions.

Something happened to me when I was on the wrong medication during my trial and error phase. I was attending an out-of-town conference, and a few of my colleagues, who I have known for 15-20 years, were at the same conference.

I was on the wrong medication for ADHD, and it was causing me to look ill and act in a strange manner. I felt horrible, and I could not correctly organize my thoughts. I do not know if it was that medication alone, or if it was the combination of it with other medication I was on at the time. Either way, it was not a good situation.

Out of concern, my colleagues questioned my health. They questioned how bad I looked, my odd behaviors, and my inability to effectively communicate with them and the students. That was very uncomfortable, and it sure did not help pave the road towards acceptance for me.

All I could tell them at the time was that I just wasn't feeling well. And today, when I look back on the situation, that was all I had to say. I strongly suspect they knew something else was at play, but it was my call to tell them or not. And I simply chose not to tell them.

I found some good information in one of the books I read to better understand and cope with my disorders. The book is called *Bipolar Disorder: A Guide for the Newly Diagnosed* by Caponigro, MA; Lee, MA; Johnson, Ph.D.; and Kring, Ph.D. They present a good way of telling people, which they call "disclosure scripts". They say to: 1) focus on the biological issues; 2) highlight the medical symptoms; 3) use caution when discussing the stigmas; and 4) let them know you are being treated (*pg. 126*).

Later in the book, they layout a "support agreement" with: 1) who you tell; 2) when you would like their help; 3) how they can help you; and 4) what you would like to hear from them (*pg. 136*). I found this to be very helpful, and I will discuss how I used these strategies with two people I have told.

I have a good friend, who is also a colleague of mine, and she knew that something was going on with me during the school year. I also knew that she was keenly aware something was not quite right with me. We had lunch one day, and I used these strategies to communicate my disorders to her.

First, I told her I was diagnosed with two biological disorders called Bipolar II and ADHD, and then I discussed how they affected me. Next, I told her that I needed her help in meetings to let me know when I appear agitated, unfocused, or disengaged.

Our agreement is that she can support me by sending me a text or giving me a signal to let me know when I display any of these types of behaviors. I do not want my colleagues, or other involved in the meeting, to think I am unprofessional or disinterested in the meeting. So, this is a great support mechanism for me now at work.

Not only did this method work well as way to share the information with her, but she was more than happy to become a part of my support team. I consider my "support team" as anyone who is aware of my disorders and is helping me through my journey. The methods presented in that book made the discussion so much easier, and it also made her feel like a trusted friend who I value, as opposed to someone I was trying to avoid for some unknown reason.

I have another colleague, and friend of over 15 years, who I also told about my disorders. He just happens to be working with some local doctors on a Bipolar Disorder study because his area of expertise is Chaos Theory. He is also my direct supervisor at work.

Since I knew he had working-knowledge about Bipolar Disorder, I knew I could skip over the parts about the stigmas. It was a more direct conversation. I also felt that, as my supervisor, he can now watch out for me and not place me on committees where he knows I might become easily agitated or unfocused.

In our discussion, he also shared with me some information about the disorder that he learned through his work in the area. So, this was another positive experience that will continue to develop overtime.

There are others in my life who I will never tell, and that includes every single member of my family. As I mentioned early on in the book, emotions are not something we talk about in my family, so being diagnosed with any psychological disorder would be considered "off-the-charts" to them.

My parents would never believe the diagnoses to be correct, they would try to convince me that I have been brainwashed, and that I am just fine. This is not what I need at this point or at any other point in my life. They would be floored that I see a therapist every week, or that I was ever sent to one in the first place for managing stress.

So, those are my stories about who I decided to share my disorders with, how I told them and why; and also those in my life I chose not to tell and why. It all boils down to building your support team on your own terms and on your own timeline.

Chapter 6:
Lack of Scientific Knowledge

This chapter focuses on the reality that, when compared to others psychological disorders, the science behind Bipolar Disorder is lagging. I explain, in a rather basic way, what is actually happening in your brain if you have this disorder. I also discuss that hope is on the horizon, as they are learning new things about the disorder all the time through research.

The Lagging Science

In some articles I have read, and in a discussion with my colleague who is working with the disorder, some proclaim that Bipolar Disorder is *the least* understood of all psychological disorders. That probably does not give you much comfort, because I know it does not provide me with much. However, progress is being made.

The National Institute of Mental Health defines Bipolar as *"unusual shifts in mood, energy, activity levels, and the ability to carry out day-to-day tasks."* That definition carries little meaning to help me understand the disorder. What do they mean by "unusual"? Also, mood, energy, activity levels, and day-to-day tasks pretty much sums up your entire day. So, all they are really saying is that Bipolar individuals are different than everyone else.

They go on to state that the disorder can range from mild to severe. So, you might be a little different from "normal" people, or you might be very different from "normal" people. The definition just does not give you much to grasp onto when you are trying to understand what is happening inside your brain and *why* you are so different.

The NIMH does have downloadable brochure on their website at (www.nimh.nih.gov) on Bipolar Disorder that discusses the symptoms, risk factors, medications, and other information. I do recommend it to anyone who needs a good starting place to learn about the disorder. But, it does not provide all the answers, primarily because they *do not exist*.

I think that those of us who have Bipolar Disorder need to become more involved rather than sitting on the sidelines. We need to be a part of the solution if we are going to learn enough about it to find better medications to control it or possibly a cure. So, at a minimum, do read about the disorder from reputable sources to learn much as you can. At the very least, you need to be an educated patient.

The fact is that the brain science behind Bipolar Disorder is just now beginning to mature. It is even possible that all areas of the brain may have something to do with the disorder. There is still so much to learn, and they are trying to discover new things every day, even as I write this book. So, part of the process is being patient, as doctors, scientists, and others attempt to uncover the true cause(s) of and cure(s) for Bipolar Disorder.

For now, I will attempt to explain some of the current science from the multiple sources that I have read in my desperate attempt to understand it. While I still do not fully understand everything, and I may not be 100% accurate, this is how I have come to comprehend the science behind what is happening inside my brain.

As of now Bipolar Disorder is classified as a psychiatric condition with extreme mood states, (sometimes called episodes), of mania and/or depression. They say "and/or", because sometimes a Bipolar person can experience both depression and mania at the same time, which is called a mixed state.

One reason that so little is known about Bipolar Disorder is because more than one part of your brain is likely involved, and doctors also believe there is not a single cause for the disorder.

Genetics do seem to play a role, as it is considered a hereditary disease. Depending on how much information you have about your family, you might be able to dig into that aspect a little more. You can try to find out, or perhaps you have witnessed, others in your family who have displayed Bipolar symptoms. I have very little information on one side of my family, so that is a bit of a dead end for me.

Next, I provide little more insight into the brain chemistry behind it, as I have grown to understand it through my various readings about the disorder. *As a disclaimer*, I do not want anyone reading this to consider it to be written by a scientist or doctor who has working knowledge of the disorder. My attempt here is to be as comprehensive and accurate as possible, but merely as someone who has the disorder and is trying to learn as much as possible to understand it.

Bipolar Disorder is considered a chemical imbalance. That is the shortened definition you will find in most of the literature. So, we need to look into it in a little more depth.

The *cerebrum* (top or main part of your brain) gathers and processes information, making connections, generating thoughts, and even controlling emotions. The *prefrontal cortex,* which is part of the cerebrum, is thought to play a major role in the emotional overreactions of someone with Bipolar Disorder. This area of the brain also seems to get the most attention in the literature, so it could be the main part of the brain creating problems for someone with the disorder.

The middle of the brain (that sits behind your temple and above your ear) is also involved. It contains the *thalamus* and *hypothalamus*. They maintain things such as sleeping, eating, and appetite, which also impact episodes and symptoms of the disorder. And, as of yet, no one knows whether the cerebellum (back of the brain near your spinal cord) plays any role in Bipolar Disorder, as its main function has more to do with complex movements.

Neurons carry signals from your brain to your body and transmit electrical impulses for chemicals to be released. Our brain needs certain chemicals to function "normally". Bipolar Disorder is the result of an imbalance in these chemicals.

There are at least two brain chemicals, or *neurotransmitters*, thought to be involved –serotonin, and dopamine. *Serotonin* helps regulate mood, anxiety, fear, sleep, body temperature, and the rate at which your body releases certain hormones. *Dopamine* is primarily linked to feelings of pleasure, and it also regulates attention and focus along with some muscle movements.

The signals being sent by the neurons are the *neurotransmitters* themselves (the chemicals of serotonin and dopamine). As mentioned, they are responsible for maintaining many things such as sleep, anxiety, fear, pleasure, and the overall regulation of your moods and hormones. But, there is a region between two neurons called the *synapse*, which is a structure that allows one neuron to pass a chemical signal to another neuron.

The *synapse* in a Bipolar individual is what prevents the two neurons from communicating properly. So what happens is that one neuron sends the signal, and the other neuron is supposed to receive it and then respond to the message with either excitement or inhibition in a "normal" manner. But, for some reason, the synapse region does not allow for this to happen properly, which leads to the mania and/or depressive mood states.

Hopefully, that description of what is occurring in your brain is somewhat helpful as is goes beyond merely providing a definition or just stating that you are different.

The Role of Your Psychiatrist

When your psychiatrist prescribes medications, he or she is ultimately trying to regulate the amount of neurotransmitters (the serotonin and/or dopamine) in your system. That is why so much of it is a crap shoot. When the doctor cannot pinpoint exactly what part(s) of the brain are involved and what neurotransmitter(s) are involved, he or she only has one choice, and that is to try out different medications to see which ones work and which ones do not work.

In my case, for example, Ambilify caused insomnia, which actually caused some hypomanic episodes. That was the opposite of what was supposed to be happening. Lamictal, on the other hand, was a drug that was working quite well to control hypomania, but it caused the side-effect of a skin rash. So, something might actually be working for the disorder but cause other problems.

This is why there is no one-size-fits-all medication for Bipolar Disorder. A certain medication may work wonders for one patient, but actually worsen the effects or causes side-effects for a different patient. Each and every patient is a completely different case, making it difficult for doctors to manage.

I remember having a conversation with an infectious disease doctor, and I asked her why she chose that field. She said that she began her medical education wanting to become an orthopedic surgeon. But then she realized that every case would be the same. Replacing a hip is replacing a hip, and she felt that overtime this would become mundane and boring. That led her to choose to become an infectious disease doctor, because every patient is a different, and each case must be analyzed and treated as unique. That is what Bipolar Disorder reminds me of when I think of how a psychiatrist must approach each patient.

You are not going in with a broken arm that simply needs to be reset and put in a cast. You are walking in with many unknown and unseen variables, providing your psychiatrist with a mystery to solve. The good news is that some doctors thrive on this, like the infectious disease doctor I discussed. You want a psychiatrist who has that kind of mindset and is willing to try new things and take things at a slow enough pace to find out what really works for *you*!

Chapter 7:
An Inside Look at Bipolar & Me

This chapter takes an in-depth look at my disorders, more specifically, how they have affected me. While I describe their impact, I do not proclaim they are the same impacts experienced by other Bipolar individuals. I will discuss how much I miss hypomania, how depression affects me, and I even share some of my dark thoughts. I also compare BPII with ADHD, because it is not uncommon to have both disorders.

I want to start by sharing an excerpt from a book,

recommended to me by my therapist, which I related to

quite well. This is from Kay Redfield Jamison's book, *An*

Unquiet Mind. The excerpt:

> *At this point in my existence, I cannot imagine*
> *leading a normal life without both taking lithium*
> *and having the benefits of psychotherapy.*
> *Psychotherapy is a sanctuary; it is a battleground; it*
> *is a place I have been psychotic, neurotic, elated,*
> *confused, and despairing beyond belief. But, always,*
> *it is where I have believed—or have learned to*
> *believe—that I might someday be able to contend*
> *with all of this." (pgs. 528-529)*

This leads me to the importance of regular psychotherapy

sessions.

The Roles of you Therapist

Despite the medications, I could not deal with any of this without a good therapist. She is the only thing that truly keeps me on path each and every week. Our sessions have also been my only hope that someday I can manage all of this and still consider myself a success.

Medications alone cannot do this for you. While they alter your mind, they do not teach you how to change your behavioral patterns and see new ways of thinking or managing your life. You need a coach, so to speak. With a good therapist, you also have safe place to discuss any or all of your thoughts and feelings. And most of all, you have accountability. My therapist provides all of these things to me. I highly recommend that you *find a good therapist* if you have been diagnosed with Bipolar Disorder!

Do not just accept any therapist. Find someone with whom you can truly acquire what I just described in the previous paragraph. I was lucky enough to find her from a past experience and the first time around. You may go through two or three before finding the right one. But trust me on this; it is well worth it, and I believe it to be an *absolute necessity*!

Missing Hypomania!

Nothing in the world beats the magic of hypomania. Your mind takes you places you never thought possible, and you can produce an enormous amount of exceptional work in no time.

Reading *An Unquiet Mind* not only helped me better understand the disorder, but it also made me realize that I am not alone in this battle. I want to share one more excerpt from Jamison's book where she describes hypomania. It is the best description that I have ever read or could ever attempt to write better. The excerpt:

> *"The countless hypomanias, and mania itself, all have brought into my life a different level of sensing and feeling and thinking. Even when I have been most psychotic—delusional, hallucinating, frenzied—I have been aware of finding new corners in my mind and heart. Some of those corners were incredible and beautiful and took my breath away and made me feel as though I could die right then and the images would sustain me. Some of them were grotesque and ugly and I never wanted to know they were there or to see them again. But, always, there were those new corners and—when feeling my normal self, beholden for that self to medicine and love—I cannot imagine becoming jaded to life, because I know of those limitless corners, with their limitless views." (pgs. 221-223)*

Hypomania is not something easily described, and even when done well, you know that the person on the other end of the conversation will never be able to fully comprehend or sense how it feels, not even your own therapist or psychiatrist.

Hypomania is something I miss on so many levels. They controlled my life, and in so many good ways. They kept me ahead of deadlines and what ultimately lead me to an endowed chair position (the top of my career-game) at a relatively young age. I have several distinguished research awards from national and international conferences and multiple journal publications that were the direct results of my hypomanic episodes.

Hypomania even kept me ahead of deadlines instead of using any type of schedule, as I was a fairly rapid-cycler, meaning I experienced hypomania often. Typically, I would have an episode about every one or two weeks.

During hypomania, the rest of the world goes away. All of your talents and thoughts center on the task at at hand, and the results are amazing. When you are in a hypomanic state, you do not need much sleep. In fact, I normally got by on about three to four hours per night, four to five nights in a row. And after each night, I felt like I had a good eight hours of sleep, which is normal for a hypomanic episode.

Sometimes at night, I would lie awake and just let all the ideas swim and self-organize in my head, and then get it on paper the next day. Other times, I would get up and start producing a research project right away, begin redesigning an entire curriculum, or work on some other project.

Nothing about it was tiresome, boring, or even energy-consuming. As fast as I can read and type, my eyes and fingers could never keep up with the ideas running through my head. And all the while I am focused on the project at hand; a separate part of my brain was organizing my schedule for the next day. It is a truly magical experience, one that anyone would want to experience.

However, not having had one in about three months now is causing some depression and other issues for me. I would take one hypomanic episode over winning the lottery at this point in time. And, that speaks volumes for how hypomania makes you feel. A huge part of me has literally died. And, I am grieving the loss of that part of me and all that it has provided me.

It is both good and bad timing now that the school year has come to an end. I do not need to rely on hypomania to get me through work deadlines. But, while I do not need it for that, I crave hypomania. I am also trying to keep myself busy without relying on hypomanic episodes to do this for me, which I have found to be quite a burden.

I am going to try and use the summer to learn more about and practice new behavioral patterns that I can utilize to get through this rough patch, and also be able to use them for my work next semester and in other areas of my life.

The yearning for hypomania is really more of a need to "feel alive again". It is a pretty humdrum life without it. Learning to make lists and calendar appointments is not very exciting. But, from what I have learned, Bipolar is a *progressive disorder* and BPII can eventually become BPI if it is not treated. It is also something you do not want to manage off and on, as this can lead to even more damage from what I understand.

I have only had one experience that could be considered full-blown mania, but it was mixed with an abundance alcohol, so I am not certain that it counts. All I know is that I do not ever care to experience something like it again. This incident happened nine or ten years ago.

My partner and I were at a heavy metal rock concert. In time, the stimulation was just too much for me to handle, with the crowd, the music, and the large outdoor the stadium. I wanted to leave, but she did not want to go with me. So, I left on my own. I had to cross a major highway to get back to where we parked.

I was so angry and over-stimulated that I stood in the middle of that highway for several seconds with a semi-truck coming straight at me. I wanted it to hit me, just to end my out of control thoughts and over-stimulated mind. Fortunately, I came to my senses in the last few seconds and finished crossing the highway.

I never even told my partner that story until recently. I do not know if it had anything to do my Bipolar Disorder, because alcohol was on board. But, I can honestly say that is the only incident I can think of where my behavior would be considered full-blown mania.

I always try to think of Bipolar I and II as one entity, just at different ranges on one continuum, because that is what it really is, even though people generally talk about BPI as being something different than BPII. My psychiatrist also believes that I have a fairly high-level of BPII, which seems to put me at an even greater risk to progress to BPI if I do not continue to treat it. That is another thing that keeps me motivated to continue with the medications instead of giving up on them just to experience hypomania.

To explain the difference in a little more detail, BPIIs experience hypomania, while BPIs experience mania. The word *"hypo"* simply means shortened, less than, or subordinated. It is a still a state of mania, but one where you are not agitated to the point of full-blown mania, meaning that you completely lose all judgment and only act on impulse, like the one I described on the highway with the semi-truck after the rock concert. Full-blown manic episodes can even be severe enough to require hospitalization.

Bipolar II can also be considered an antecedent to Bipolar I, which is why it is considered a progressive disorder. To me, this is quite disconcerting. And according to the National Institute of Mental Health, Bipolar Disorder tends to worsen over time if left untreated. Knowing that makes me even more committed to staying on my treatment path.

Depression – The Other Side of Hypomania

While the euphoric state of hypomania lies on one end of the disorder, depression lies on the other end. I talked about experiencing depression in graduate school, but I really did not know what it was then. I do now, but I experience it in somewhat different manners than most descriptions I have found in the literature or in how they depict it on TV commercials.

When depression takes its toll after hypomania ends, all my energy is completely gone. I feel entirely worthless. So, I go from one extreme to the other, where I have all the vigor in the world to make magical things happen, to sitting on the couch feeling like I have no value in this world.

It does not even feel like a state of sadness, as people describe what "feeling sad" is supposed to be like. I do not get tearful. I just feel like I have no worth. Sometimes I have dark thoughts like wishing I was the one who had died of cancer instead of my brother, and wondering why God took him over me. He was a better person in my eyes, plus he had children.

I do not feel physical aches and pains. I never feel like staying in bed all day. If anything, I would rather grab the loaded .38 revolver on my nightstand and put a bullet in my head than lie there any longer with my thoughts. I simply want to *escape my own presence*. Dying just seems like the only way out sometimes.

The Disappearing Act

Well before my diagnosis, I literally started to think of a way to just disappear. I felt my problems were all coming from everything around me and all the decisions I had made. So, if I could just get away from everything, all the problems would disappear too.

In my profession, you can find a job in just about anywhere the world. So, I started searching for professorship positions in my area of expertise. They were all over the globe. It would be so easy to find a job at a college or university just under the radar, and in a fairly interesting area of the world, like New Zealand, to simply start a brand new life.

My plan was to find a mediocre college, make living teaching classes, and become a recluse. I would disappear in the summer between school years and not tell a single person where I was going or that I was even leaving. This would be a completely brand new start for me, and all my depression and problems would go away.

I went as far as searching for jobs and even pinpointed a few. But, I never even began to apply for any of them. I think that step was halted by the mere selfish nature of the plan. My parents had already lost one child, my partner needs me on several levels, plus anyone who cares for me would never have any closure. Along with that, I love my partner too much to be without her.

Now that I know my problems are internally bound due to my disorders, this plan no longer lingers in my head, as now it makes no sense. But, it does resurface as a little fantasy from time-to-time when I need an escape from a rough day.

The Need to Hurt Others

Sometimes, I feel the need to hurt others as well, especially when I feel victimized or like I might be victimized. Our house has been broken into twice. The first time was in the middle of the night and we were home. Luckily, our dog attacked him and he fled. That man is now on death row for murder. I even had to testify in his sentencing trial. Even though nothing really happened to us that night, I still want to watch him die, mainly because of the horrible things he did to others, and would have done to us, if it were not for our brave dog.

The second time our house was broken into was in the middle of the day. Someone took several hits and kicks at our front door and knocked it in on a Friday afternoon. They made it out with our jewelry boxes. Sometimes I find myself wishing I were home that day, so when that door came flying open, I was there ready to put a bullet through his brain. My brother always taught me to shoot at the head, chest, and then head again. Those are the three shots I think about taking when I suffer episodes of depression.

I don't really "feel" angry. I simply remember back on real-life situations or think of possible instances where someone might try to victimize me or my family, and I am there to kill them. In reality, I do not really want to hurt or kill anyone. And it is not something I think about at any other time, but that is how anger exposes itself when I am depressed.

To me, my depression seems more like some sort of a cognitive exercise than an emotional response to things around me, much like thinking through those kinds of dreadful situations and how I would handle them.

Suicidal Thoughts

I would never commit suicide, but I do think about it from time to time. I have a loaded .38 within arm's reach of where I lay my head at night. But, if I were to do it, there would be no room for error. I would use my .38 inside the mouth and my partner's 9mm to the temple. I would not mess around with trying to overdose on drugs or take it beyond my own household, where sometimes you hear of people jumping off of bridges.

I would clear out the room of all furniture and other items to not leave such a mess for others to find or clean up. While such as well thought-out plan is often a "red flag" for a potential suicide attempt, I would not go through with it. But, with all that has come forth over the past year, you cannot blame me for having such a plan should things worsen.

Again, I do not think I am capable of committing suicide. For one, my partner needs me too much. Secondly, I could not do that to my dogs. That may sound a little silly, but I could not leave them like that or have them witness such an awful thing. Nor could I leave my parents with a second child who has died. I saw, firsthand, what the loss of a child did to them. I cannot imagine what that kind of experience would leave them to handle. And from my religious beliefs, I do not think that is what God wants for me.

ADHD Coupled with Bipolar Disorder

As terrible as the word "comorbid" sounds, it means that two or more conditions co-exist. I was diagnosed with both ADHD and Bipolar II, which apparently is not uncommon.

Attention-Deficit/Hyperactive Disorder is characterized by inattention, hyperactivity, and impulsiveness. That leads to an inability to focus, being disorganized, forgetfulness, and also becoming restless. These symptoms are also present with Bipolar Disorder too. So, what is the difference?

From what I understand, ADHD symptoms tend to last all day, while Bipolar symptoms cycle on and off.

ADHD also occurs with small "triggers", like a person in meeting who will not stop talking, so you disengage because you simply cannot bear to listen to him or her talk any longer. With Bipolar Disorder, mood shifts can come and go without any triggers or due to larger triggers, such as having a stressful day. So, you may already be in a mood state going into a meeting that predisposes you to disengagement and a lack of focus throughout meeting, regardless of who is speaking or on what topic.

Another difference is that ADHD is more behavioral in nature, while Bipolar has more to do with your mood state. This may seem easier to grasp on paper, but when you are in the midst of experiencing something like an inability to focus during a meeting, it is difficult to know whether it is being caused by ADHD or Bipolar Disorder.

Take the example I provided in a previous chapter about the fact that it takes me three to four hours to pack for a weekend trip. I am not sure if that has more to do with my ADHD, Bipolar Disorder, or possibly both are at play in some way.

Bipolar individuals are also more likely to self-medicate, such as drinking alcohol to slow down the number of ideas and thoughts filtering through the mind, while this is more unlikely for ADHD individuals. That is what I was previously doing to help control my mood states and put my mind at ease before I stopped drinking and gave into the medications.

If you do not have a reputable psychiatrist who is skilled and experienced with diagnosing and treating both disorders, you might walk away with the wrong diagnosis. And, treating both of them together is another complexity. From what I understand, a drug that helps control ADHD may worsen symptoms of Bipolar Disorder and vice versa. So finding the right psychiatrist is *absolutely essential* for diagnosing and managing one or both of these disorders.

I am on medications for both disorders, and as of now, they are working fairly well. So, I try not to spend too much time trying to figure it all out. I just know that I have both conditions and they require medication and therapy.

My psychiatrist referred a book to me called *Driven to Distraction* by Hollowell, M.D. and Ratey, M.D. It helped me better understand ADHD, both in recognizing the symptoms and using different coping mechanisms. However, I still find it hard to distinguish between BPII and ADHD when I am in the middle of a situation where I am feeling agitated, impatient, or just unable to focus. I hope this gets better with time and experience.

Chapter 8:
Dealing with All the "Other" Issues

As you stumble through the darkness of trying to deal with your Bipolar Disorder, you are going to run into a few other problems. Some will be scarier than others, and some will leave bigger scars than others. This chapter focuses on the trials and tribulations of trying different medications, the cost of good health care, battling your insurance company, and it also takes an even closer look at the disorder from my viewpoint.

The Medication Rollercoaster

As I mentioned in the introduction of this book, the amount of information available on Bipolar Disorder is somewhat limited, as the science is behind the times when compared to other psychological disorders. It is sort of a shot-gun approach to see which medications work and which do not work. This can be aggravating, in and of itself, and that alone can make you want to give up. I have been completely deflated because of it. So, I will describe my medication roller coaster ride.

Once my initial diagnoses were complete, I was prescribed four medications – Ambien for sleep, Klonopin for social anxiety, Lamitcal for BPII, and Vyvanse for ADHD. I was already on Ambien and Klonopin from my general practitioner. The other two were new.

On both of these new medications, you have to start off at low dosages and gradually increase them. As with all medications, they come with side-effects. At first, I was doing well with both, along with no side-effects. But that changed.

One of the side effects of Lamictal, used for treating Bipolar Disorder, is a skin rash, and there are two types. One type is fairly benign and the other can be fatal. I started Lamitcal at a 25mg dosage, and once I reached a 150mg dosage, I broke out into a rash. Fortunately, it was the benign type. But, that still meant no more Lamictal, which was working well to control hypomania.

The second medication she prescribed was Abilify. One side-effect can be insomnia, which was the case for me. Even with my Ambien on board, it would still keep me up at night, throwing me into hypomania, which defeated the whole purpose of the medication.

So, we tried a third medication called Saphris. It is something you take at night that also works as a sedative. After being on Saphris for almost three months now, I have not had one hypomanic episode. So, the medication works and with no side-effects. But, this whole process took six months before finding Saphris.

Before finding Vyvanse for ADHD, I was on a drug called Focalin. This drug did not work for me at all. On the medication, I could not correctly organize my thoughts. My speech pattern was slowed, and sometimes I did not make much sense. My therapist quickly picked-up on this in my sessions. I even forgot to pay some of my bills during the month I was on it.

I do not know if it was that medication alone or in combination with other medications that caused this, but it was making my life and symptoms worse, not better. In fact, when I think back on it, I really do not think I should have even been operating a motor vehicle while on it.

Insurance Company Battles

So, I finally found a medication that works for my Bipolar Disorder, Saphris, and my insurance company denied coverage. I was so angry and in such a state of confusion, that I experienced a very bad state of depression, one of my all-time lows. I even had suicidal thoughts, just because I did not want to be dealing with any or all of this anymore.

My psychiatrist called the insurance company to file an appeal, and they denied her claim. As a patient, I filed an appeal as well. So far, my appeal has also been denied until I send in all my medical records, including those from my general practitioner. And even then, they have to go over everything again before making a decision, which could still result in a denial.

All the other medications out that I have not tried cause weight gain. And, as I mentioned before, weight gain is not an option for my physical health reasons alone. So, I need to stay on Saphris. But, one really good thing came from the next appointment to see my psychiatrist.

She knows Saphris is the right medication for me, and she promised to keep me supplied with samples of it as long as I promised to stay on it. This provides a great deal of relief, and I have even more confidence and trust in her as my doctor. This is a great example of good quality healthcare.

But, I also know in the back of my mind, that if I lose her for any reason, then I lose the Saphris too. My therapist is trying to get me not to focus on that possibility, but instead, focus on the positive and present. I do not do that very well, as I naturally tend to worry about the future.

Now for the next blow! My insurance company also cut me off of Vyvanse for my ADHD, and it was working wonders. In fact, right after the appointment when my psychiatrist and I felt that we had found the perfect dosage, I received the news. With Vyvanse, I started off with a 20mg dosage and we were slowly increasing it. I was at a dosage of 120mg, and we were going to bump it up a tad more to 140mg when I was cut-off.

Vyvanse pills come in maximum dosages of 70mg per pill, but my insurance company will not fund two pills per day. Luckily, my doctor figured out a way to supplement what I was lacking in the dosage needed. I now take 60mg of Adderall on top of the 70mg of Vyvanse, and both are covered by insurance. This seems to be working okay so far, but I saw better results with Vyvanse alone.

I can go to an external review board in my state if my insurance company ends up denying Saphris and Vyvanse all together. If the external review board also denies them, then I just have to hope to get my Saphris from my psychiatrist as long as possible and also hope that the Vyvanse and Adderall continue to work together fairly well.

There is also the chance that other medications will become available in the near future as the result of current and future research. So, I try to think that some hope may be on the horizon.

The Cost if Quality Healthcare

You cannot put a price on good health, but know that finding and maintaining good quality healthcare will cost money. Your psychiatrist appointments, therapy sessions, and medications all require money. You must be willing to devote the funds necessary to make sure you receive good quality care.

Even if your insurance covers part of it, there will be some out-of-pocket expenses. In my case, my health insurance plan covers most of my medication expenses and my co-pay for my psychiatric appointments is relatively low. However, my psychotherapy sessions are not covered by my insurance. This holds true for both my partner and me. However, I would never seek out another therapist. As I mentioned before, it is about quality of life, and my therapist provides many things to me that I would not try to change or even attempt to find in another therapist.

There may be things you need to give up for good healthcare in exchange for the services and medications you are receiving. For example, my partner and I quit drinking, which was a huge expense every month when you add up the costs of all the drinks at home and out to dinner. In fact, we spend less on our mental healthcare bills combined than we used to spend on alcohol. While that seems incredible to believe, it is true.

So, it might be helpful for you to consider some things you can give up in exchange for better healthcare. Chances are, if you are suffering from Bipolar Disorder, you are also engaging in some kind of substance abuse. Giving up the cost of that substance just might cover the cost of good, high-quality mental healthcare.

Even if it is not substance abuse you need to give up, there are probably other things in your life worth giving up that are just not as important. Money is a factor that you need to account for, and do not sacrifice quality to save a few bucks. Your health is way too important, as it impacts all other aspects of your life.

Genetic Testing

I was fortunate enough to have some genetic testing done through my psychiatrist. This was performed to see what specific medications my body responds to best and also how my body metabolizes medication. Fortunately, my doctor's office was in a group for some trial studies, so I did not have to pay for this service.

The results were of great value. For one, I found out that I am an "ultra-metabolizer". This basically means that I need higher dosages of medication than your average person. So, if the dosages of any of the medications I mentioned before seem high, that is why. My body just metabolizes medication quickly.

It also showed what medications I do not respond to well, such as Lexapro. My general practitioner had me on this common drug for depression, but I was able to get off of it, not only because I do not respond well to it, but because I now have other medications on board.

At least I have that report to help all my doctors and me know what medications my body will respond to better than others. And I also know that I will need higher dosages of medication than most people because of how fast my body metabolizes it.

There is not a one-size-fits-all prescription for Bipolar Disorder. It is a trial and error process that one must be willing to go through. And that is one of the most frustrating things about it, along with the fact that the Bipolar mindset is not built to deal with that kind of frustration, especially when coupled with ADHD like me.

Then, you may have to battle your insurance company like I am currently doing. That is another detailed process that neither fits the mind of a Bipolar or ADHD individual. But, I keep the "quality of life" discussions I have had with my therapist in mind. And I know have to fight for myself, because no one else can do it for me.

Perhaps I can win the fight against my insurance company, but perhaps not. In the meantime, I just have to focus on the present, take my medications, try to make some behavioral progress every day, and continue working with my therapist to make other necessary changes in to mindset and life.

My Talents Despite My Disorder

On some websites and in some books, they try to make you feel better by listing off famous authors, actors, inventors, or important historians who may have had or do have Bipolar Disorder. While that may make some people feel better, it does nothing for me. But I have to admit that sometimes I question how much of the disorder is really "bad" and how much of it I really want to completely dissolve through medication.

There is a book that many organizations use called *StrengthsFinder 2.0*. It was developed by the Gallup Organization, and it has outstanding statistical validity and reliability to determine what one's top-five strengths are from 34 possibilities. It was also a *#1 Wall Street Journal* and *#1 Business Week* bestseller.

The original database was developed by using over 100,000 people, and today this tool is utilized in more than 100 countries, in 20 different languages, and by more companies than you can imagine for selecting people to hire and for putting together work teams. My top-five strengths summarized include:

- *Intellection* – introspective and needs to be alone frequently. Anxiety over the future. New ideas in mind most of the time.

- *Maximizer* – needs to take something strong and make it superb. Trusts instincts and talents to progress over time and move faster.

- *Deliberative* – driven by talents and must see success over time before calling it a success. Typically remains silent over personal information.

- *Strategic* – needs to understand how things work. Sees alternative paths and patterns others generally do not see. Generates innovative ideas before proceeding.

- *Learner* – needs to know everything about everything. Driven by talents and likely to be self-taught in many ways. Desires to learn more and improve.

One day, while I was discussing the *StrengthsFinder* assessment with my students, and I began to re-look at my own top-five strengths. Looking at each one alone provided little insight into my Bipolar Disorder. But, when I began to look at them in combination, I could see Bipolar II written all over them. The blending of the strengths seems to describe my hypomanic states quite well.

Three of them refer to being more introspective, three others about generating ideas and learning more, two about being very purposeful in creating outstanding outcomes of your work, and one even includes feelings of anxiety.

I believe that these strengths are a part of me all of the time, but they are in *pure overdrive* during hypomania. I can even make a sentence out of the five strengths for when I am in a hypomanic state.

My <u>intellectual</u> capacity and desire to <u>learn</u>
allows me to <u>deliberately maximize</u> my efforts,
so that I can <u>strategically</u> find ways of doing things
that no one else can do better than me.

To me, this is what it means to be productive.

Anything less than achieving the ultimate goal of that

sentence is just time spent working. Being *productive* is

what makes me truly happy, not just working.

While I cringe at the thought of public recognition, I

am very proud of the distinguished research awards I have

received over the years. I am proud to see the results of my

work cited in others' textbooks and journal articles. To me

production means the outstanding outcomes of the work

that you do.

The things that make a difference in your field and

the differences you make in the world are the only things

that matter. Work for the sake of work is meaningless. But,

that is just how I feel about myself and life in general.

In a sense, I see my strengths as my purpose, which is why it gives me so much anguish to realize they are also such a huge part of my disorder. I need to spend some time thinking about how I want to view this and what I want to do with this information. As of now, I am truly at a loss, which is causing some major issues and internal struggles for me right now.

Is Bipolar Disorder Really a Disorder?

Disorder means chaos, confusion, turmoil, and mayhem. All of those words have bad connotations. Ask most people, and they do not want to live in such a state. Look at my desk and all you see is mayhem. Look into my mind, and all you can find is chaos.

I am easily confused over things most people find to be common-sense. Most of the time, I feel I am in a state of turmoil just trying to get through the day without forgetting a meeting, running an errand, or fulfilling a minor obligation, such as putting gas in my car that other people simply find routine.

My partner refers to me as "a mess". She does most of the household chores, because I find them somewhat intimidating. I cannot seem to do them right as proclaimed by my mother as a child and my partner as an adult. For example, what is the purpose of folding a fitted sheet? You roll it up and stick it on the shelf. Once you put it on the bed, the wrinkles go away.

I cannot find the patience to stack bowls and pans from biggest to smallest in the cabinet. Just throw it in there. It is in a 2'x3' space somewhere, so it will not be that hard to find when you need it. Thankfully, my partner does leave my office alone though, as that is my sanctuary. She definitely knows better than to mess with my piles of disarray.

My office has stacks and stacks of different papers, sometimes mixed with books, Post-it Notes, receipts, or other forms of information. And while the stacks make no sense to anyone else, somehow they make sense to me. I know what project is in what pile, and about how far down in the pile to start looking when I need some information.

My office at school is the same, but I hide it. I have six file drawers, two at each of my desks and an extra one in the corner. Not one file exists in any of those file drawers. They are my stacks. My secretary calls them my "pile drawers". But, I have my students convinced that I am somewhat organized.

This is what makes being Bipolar II, along with ADHD, so difficult to see as entirely bad or something you want to completely nullify. Under hypomania, you produce exceptional work. No one can beat you when you are in that state of mind. And that is what makes it difficult to accept as a "disorder" or mental illness. Disorder just means there is a lack of order to it. Why is order so important if you can do it better under disorder?

But where and when does it stop? And *that* is the problem with Bipolar being a *progressive* disorder. How will you know when you are about to go from hypomania to full-blown mania if left untreated?

That leads back to the *physiology* that is occurring in the brain. With too much disorder, there is no judgment and too many things can be done or said out of pure impulse that can be very destructive, not only to you, but others around you. I think back to my one-time possible occurrence with pure mania and the semi-truck. My mind was in such a state of turmoil, that I almost lost my life that night. I do not ever want to experience anything like that again.

So, if I accept my Bipolar II diagnosis without treatment and leave it to chance that it progresses to Bipolar I, then what would happen? While that is an unknown factor, it is a possibility. And I do not I want to take that gamble, especially with the current lack of knowledge in the field.

My psychiatrist also likes to remind me of the downsides to hypomania. Those include the racing thoughts that do not allow me to settle down enough to sleep or complete simple tasks, becoming irritable, being easily agitated, and becoming so focused on something that I am unable to have a simple conversation with my partner. These are all true, and they do cause problems for me. But, I sure do miss the highs of hypomania. However, I also realize that not all good things come from it.

So, now to answer to the question in the title of this section, is Bipolar Disorder really a "disorder"? The answer is "yes" for now. It is not something you want to take lightly, even if you are pinpointed fairly low on the Bipolar spectrum. Right now, there is just not enough scientific knowledge behind it to treat it otherwise.

Chapter 9:
The Future

When I think of both Bipolar II and ADHD as lifelong illnesses I have to manage forever, sometimes it literally makes me fearful, and other times it makes me quite angry. It is just so unsettling to think about having these disorders that I must now manage forever. But it is my reality, and one that I must accept as a big part of my life now.

I was one of those people who never wanted to be on any medication for anything. Who does? Now, I am on medication forever, and five different kinds to control my Bipolar, ADHD, social anxiety, and sleep disorder. Sometimes I find myself feeling defiant when I have to take the medications. But, I know they are a necessity.

I have forgotten to take my ADHD medications a couple of times. That is not something I want to experience again. The medications are on board to manage your brain activity, which affects everything throughout your day. Without them, everything becomes unmanageable and unbearable.

I know I will be in therapy for a long while. As I mentioned before, the accountability alone issue is a major issue for me right now. Without my weekly appointments, I would not be where I am today and might not be on board at all with managing my disorders. Plus, it is the only place I can get everything sorted out and make a plan for the week, along with setting some long-term goals. I go on Mondays, which I like, because it gets the week started off on the right foot.

While I initially find myself rejecting some of the new behavioral strategies we discuss in our sessions, I know I have to get on board with them. I do not know what it is like to sit on the other side of the table from me, but I would like to experience that sometime.

I listen and do try, but sometimes I feel like I should be progressing faster. For example, I still do not have a packing list for my work trips like she asked me to make about two trips ago. However, she once told me I am doing the best I can under all the things that have occurred over the past year.

And when I think back on this past year, and all the struggles my partner and I have dealt with, I am amazed at how well we are doing. I am not even sure that most couples would still be together. My partner initially went in for therapy for her alcoholism, which ultimately led to my comorbid diagnoses of BPII and ADHD, all within just a few months of each other. We use humor much of the time to get through our issues, and fortunately, we are both committed to sobriety for the long-term.

I could not be more proud of her and her abstinence from alcohol, especially in light of my unforeseen diagnoses. There are some days I know am not there for her at all. But, she has more internal strength than anyone I have ever known, so I know she will continue down the right path.

My support team, as of now, consists of my therapist, my psychiatrist, my partner, and two friends, who are also colleagues. I am not sure at this point who else to tell, if anyone. But for now, things are going okay. I have so much more to learn, and I still have some major struggles to overcome.

Bipolar Disorder and ADHD are my battles to fight, but also I feel that I need to become part of the solution. That is why I wanted to write this book, to tell my story as a possible way to help others. There are very few books out there where people are willing to tell their story, mainly because of the stigmas and the dark sides attached to the disorder. They are not only difficult to come to terms with yourself, but they are extremely hard to reveal even to your closest confidants.

Moreover, I do not want to be just one more diagnosed patient who just sits on sidelines waiting for things to happen. I want to try to make some kind of positive difference, if even for just one person. There is nothing I can do about the science, or lack thereof. But, I do know they are trying to make progress, and I plan to keep up with it, as should you.

If you are struggling with Bipolar Disorder, I hope that at least some, or my entire story and resources I shared, helped you in some way. All of us who are struggling with the disorder have different stories to tell and different ways of dealing with it. But, I will conclude with a short list of things I think all of us should consider:

1. Realize you are not alone, as it is estimated that 5.7 million American adults have this disorder, according to the NIMH (www.nimh.hin.gov).

2. Tell yourself that you did *not* cause the disorder and that you are *not* the disorder. The disorder is a physiological condition that you have and did not create, much like someone diagnosed with type I Diabetes.

3. Do not give up, despite all the other obstacles, like medication trial-and-errors, healthcare costs, and insurance battles.

4. Stay on your medications and listen to your psychiatrist and your therapist's advice. Consider them to be the foundation of your support team.

5. Create the rest of your support team on your own terms and on your own timeline. Also, remember that not everyone has to know about your disorder.

6. While the science to date has lagged in comparison to other psychological disorders, realize that progress is being made in the field to better understand and treat those of us with Bipolar Disorder. And who knows, someday there may even be a cure!

REFERENCES

An Unquiet Mind: A Memoir of Moods and Madness. (1996). Jamison, K.R. Vintage Books: Random House Publishing.

Bipolar Disorder: A Guide for the Newly Diagnosed. (2013). Caponigro, J.M., Lee, E.H., Johnson, and Kring, A.M. New Harbinger Pulibcations.

Driven to Distraction. (2011). Hallowell, E.M., and Ratey, J.J. Anchor Books.

The National Institute of Mental Health. (http:www.nimh.hin.gov/; accessed May 2013)

Quiet: the Power of Introverts in a World that Can't Stop Talking. (2012). Cain, S. Crown Publishing.

StregthsFinder2.0. (www.strengthsfinder.com; accessed May 2013)

www.ingramcontent.com/pod-product-compliance
Lightning Source LLC
Chambersburg PA
CBHW030447290526
45786CB00001B/477